A Guide for Using

Out of the Dust

in the Classroom

Based on the novel by Karen Hesse

This guide written by Sarah Kartchner Clark, M.A.

Teacher Created Materials, Inc.
6421 Industry Way
Westminster, CA 92683
www.teachercreated.com
©*1999 Teacher Created Materials*
Reprinted, 2003
Made in U.S.A.
ISBN 1-57690-623-X

Edited by
Barbara Wally, M.S.

Illustrated by
Wendy Chang

Cover Art by
Wendy Chang/Agi Palinay

Table of Contents

Introduction 3

Sample Lesson Plans 4

Before the Book (*Pre-reading Activities*) 5

About the Author 6

Book Summary 7

Vocabulary Lists 8

Vocabulary Activities 9

Section 1 (*Pages 1–51*) 10
- Show What You Know!
- Hands-on Project—*Apple Recipes*
- Cooperative Learning Activity—*Creative Problem Solving*
- Curriculum Connection—*Math: Startling Statistics*
- Into Your Life—*Reading Response Journals*

Section 2 (*Pages 52–95*) 15
- Show What You Know!
- Hands-on Project—*Depression Details*
- Cooperative Learning Activity—*Characterization*
- Curriculum Connection—*Language Arts: In the News*
- Into Your Life—*Through Our Own Eyes*

Section 3 (*Pages 96–149*) 20
- Show What You Know!
- Hands-on Project—*The 3-D Effect*
- Cooperative Learning Activity—*Create-a-Story*
- Curriculum Connection—*Social Studies: Map of Oklahoma*
- Into Your Life—*Compare and Contrast*

Section 4 (*Pages 150–189*) 25
- Show What You Know!
- Hands-on Project—*Posters with Pizzazz!*
- Cooperative Learning Activity—*Wind Erosion*
- Curriculum Connection—*Science/Health: Dust Pneumonia*
- Into Your Life—*In the Book or My Life?*

Section 5 (*Pages 190–227*) 30
- Show What You Know!
- Hands-on Project—*Character Cube*
- Cooperative Learning Activity—*Lights, Camera, Action!*
- Curriculum Connection—*Language Arts: Writing in Free Verse*
- Into Your Life—*Forgiveness*

After the Book (*Post-reading Activities*) 35
- Research Activity
- Book Report Ideas
- A New Twist

Culminating Activities 38
- Memories from the Dust Game
- Letter to Karen Hesse

Unit Test Options 43

Bibliography of Related Reading 46

Answer Key 47

Introduction

Literature opens the door to magical new worlds. By engaging our imaginations and emotions, books allow us to learn about people we may never meet and explore places we may never go. The best books also help us discover more about ourselves. Like a good friend, a good book touches and enriches our lives forever.

In *Literature Units*, great care has been taken to select books that are sure to become good friends!

Teachers who use this literature unit will find the following features to supplement their own valuable ideas:

- Sample Lesson Plans
- Pre-reading Activities
- A Biographical Sketch and Picture of Author
- A Book Summary
- Vocabulary Lists and Suggested Vocabulary Activities
- Chapters grouped for study with each section including the following:
    - *a quiz*
    - *a hands-on project*
    - *a cooperative learning activity*
    - *a cross-curricular connection*
    - *an extension into the reader's life*

- Post-reading Activities
- Research Ideas
- Book Report Ideas
- Culminating Activities
- Three Different Options for Unit Tests
- Bibliography of Related Reading
- Answer Key

Using this unit as part of your teaching strategy can help you show your students how reading can touch their lives in wondrous ways.

Sample Lesson Plans

Each of the lessons suggested below can take from one to several days to complete.

Lesson 1
- Introduce and complete some or all of the pre-reading activities, page 5.
- Read "About the Author" with your students, page 6.
- Introduce the vocabulary list for Section 1, page 8.

Lesson 2
- Read Section 1 of *Out of the Dust* (pages 1–51). As you read, place the vocabulary words in the context of the story and discuss their meanings.
- Choose a vocabulary activity, page 9.
- Try "Apple Recipes," page 11.
- Complete "Creative Problem Solving" page 12.
- Do the graphing activity on unemployment during the Depression, page 13.
- Begin "Reading Response Journals," page 14.
- Administer the Section 1 quiz, page 10.
- Introduce the vocabulary list for Section 2, page 8.

Lesson 3
- Read Section 2 of *Out of the Dust* (pages 52–95). As you read, place the vocabulary words in the context of the story and discuss their meanings.
- Choose a vocabulary activity, page 9.
- Assign projects from "Depression Details," page 16.
- Do the characterization exercises, page 17.
- Write a newspaper article, page 18.
- Learn the stages of grief, page 19.
- Administer the Section 2 quiz, page 15.
- Introduce the vocabulary list for Section 3, page 8.

Lesson 4
- Read Section 3 of *Out of the Dust* (pages 96–149). As you read, place the vocabulary words in the context of the story and discuss their meanings.
- Choose a vocabulary activity, page 9.
- Make a 3-D picture, page 21.

- Work with a group to write a story, page 22.
- Complete the mapping activity, page 23.
- Compare and contrast your life with that of the main character, page 24.
- Administer the Section 3 quiz, page 20.
- Introduce the vocabulary list for Section 4, page 8.

Lesson 5
- Read Section 4 of *Out of the Dust* (pages 150–189). As you read, place the vocabulary words in the context of the story and discuss their meanings.
- Choose a vocabulary activity, page 9.
- Make a poster, page 26.
- Complete the "Wind Erosion" Experiment, page 27.
- Label the lung diagram, page 28.
- Compare experiences in your life to the book, page 29.
- Administer the Section 4 quiz, page 25.
- Introduce the vocabulary list for Section 5, page 8.

Lesson 6
- Read Section 5 of *Out of the Dust* (pages 190–227). As you read, place the vocabulary words in the context of the story and discuss their meanings.
- Choose a vocabulary activity, page 9.
- Make the "Character Cube," page 31.
- Produce a play, page 32.
- Learn to write in free verse, page 33.
- Explore the importance of forgiveness, page 34.
- Administer the Section 5 quiz, page 30.

Lesson 7
- Assign research projects, book reports, and "A New Twist," pages 35–38.
- Begin work on culminating activities, pages 38–42.

Lesson 8
- Administer Unit Tests 1, 2, and/or 3, pages 43–45.
- Provide a list of related reading materials for your students, page 46.

Before the Book

Before students begin reading *Out of the Dust,* have them do some pre-reading activities to stimulate interest and enhance their comprehension of this award-winning book.

- Spread dishes, farm tools, books, and other items out on a table. Bring in a bucket full of sand and sprinkle some over these items. Leave the bucket of sand on the table. Ask students to write a story about the items they see on the table. Share these stories as a class.

- As a class, watch the PBS video *The Great Depression.* See the bibliography on page 46 for information on how to get this video. Discuss the students' thoughts and feelings about this time period.

- Divide the class into cooperative learning groups to research and write a report together on the Dust Bowl or the Great Depression in American history.

- Show pictures from the book *Children of the Dust Bowl: The True Story of the School at Weedpatch Camp* by Jerry Stanley. Discuss with your students what life would be like and how the people are feeling in these pictures. These pictures could be used on a bulletin board display in your classroom.

- Ask the students to consider the following questions.
  - Have you ever been involved in a serious accident? What happened?
  - What is your relationship like with your parents? Can you confide in them? Are they easy to talk to?
  - Have you ever lost a parent?
  - What are your talents? Make a mental list of them.
  - How does weather affect our lives?
  - Have you ever been in a serious storm? What happened?
  - What are your goals in life? What are you doing to accomplish them?
  - What do you know about the President of the United States? Do you like him? Why or why not?

- Distribute copies of *Out of the Dust.* Have students look at the cover and title. What does the title mean? Have students predict what they think the story will be about.

- Explain to the students that the book is written in free verse, a modern form of poetry that has variable lines with no rhyming pattern and no set rhythm. Read them some examples of free verse and explain that *Out of the Dust* is written in free verse, rather than in paragraphs.

About the Author

Karen Hesse is an author with the ability to inspire and motivate readers to tackle difficult topics. Many of her books deal with difficult issues. She has written three historical fiction books and loves the connection to the past that this format provides.

Her work includes books entitled *Wish on a Unicorn, The Music of the Dolphins, A Time of Angels, Phoenix Rising,* and *Letters from Rifka.* She has also written books for younger children including *Sable, Poppy's Chair, Lavender,* and *Lester's Dog. Out of the Dust* received the Newbery Medal of Honor for 1998.

Hesse was born and raised in Baltimore, Maryland. Married at the age of 19, she now makes her home in Vermont with her husband Randy and daughters Kate and Rachel. Hesse's editor describes her as empathetic, quiet, and humble, yet a born performer in front of an audience. Her books show that she loves the land, values independence, and feels that family is important.

Hesse began her writing efforts with poetry. With two small children to nurture, she found it hard to focus on poetry and turned to literature. Explaining why she chose to write the story *Out of the Dust* in free verse, she said, "I never attempted to write this book any other way than in free verse. The frugality of the life, the hypnotically hard work of farming, the grimness of conditions during the dust bowl demanded an economy of words. Daddy and Ma and Billie Jo's rawboned life translated into poetry. . . ."

The inspiration for *Out of the Dust* came from a visit to Kansas during which Hesse experienced a tornado. These experiences in the Midwest were the beginnings of a story centered in the Dust Bowl of the Great Depression. Karen Hesse did many hours of research with the aid of the Oklahoma Historical Society to create validity and accuracy in her retelling of this trying and demanding time in our country's history. Karen hopes that young adults reading this story will come away with a sense of the desperation of the times and of how forgiveness affects our everyday lives.

Out of the Dust

by Karen Hesse
(Scholastic, 1997)
(available in CAN, Scholastic; UK, Scholastic Limited; AUS, Ashton Scholastic Propriety Ltd.)

Out of the Dust is a series of free-verse poems written by Karen Hesse. Billie Jo, the main character, relates the trials and struggles of growing up on a wheat farm in Oklahoma during the Dust Bowl years of the Great Depression. This touching novel conveys the heat, dust, and wind of Oklahoma that tore at the farmland and hearts of the people.

Billie Jo is a red-haired, talented, young pianist who happens to love apples. She is also excited about the expected arrival of a new baby in their family. Billie Jo will almost be 14 by the time the baby is born. She knows her daddy wants a boy.

Because of her musical talent, Billie Jo is asked by Arley Wanderdale to perform with the Black Mesa Boys at various events in the community. She is thrilled at these opportunities, but sometimes Ma does not let her go. These piano performances take her out of her sometimes-miserable life in the Dust Bowl and put her into a world of excitement, wonder, and music.

Growing up during the Depression, Billie Jo experiences the darkness of the times. With her dad's crops failing, Billie Jo and her expectant mother are also involved in a tragic accident that changes Billie Jo's life forever. She is left without a mother and without the ability to play the piano. In addition to this, Billie Jo and her father have grown more distant  and seldom talk since the deaths of her mother and her baby brother. As she struggles to work on a relationship with a distant father, Billie Jo feels as though she is drowning in the dust.

One night in desperation she catches a train and runs away from home. She spends the night talking to a homeless man about his family. After reaching Flagstaff, Arizona, Billie Jo decides to return home and face the life she left behind.

Back home, Billie Jo reaches a turning point in her life. As she and her dad walk back home from town, they both realize that changes need to take place for them to survive. Daddy promises to have the spots on his skin checked, and Billie Jo decides to stretch her scarred hands across the keys of the piano again.

Louise, a friend of Daddy's, enters their lives at the end of the story, bringing new light, new hope, and a new future. Billie Jo slowly learns to open up, love, forgive, and trust again.

Vocabulary Lists

On this page are vocabulary lists that correspond to each sectional grouping. Vocabulary activity ideas can be found on page 9 of this book.

Section 1
Pages 1–51

bittering	dazzled	pestering	riled	slants
bounty	fidgeting	pledged	rippling	sorghum
cast-off	fingerwork	plowboy	roughs	spindly
dazed	oilcloth	ratcheted	scowling	wisp

Section 2
Pages 52–95

cereus	desperate	obliged	sod	trickling
chafed	floorboards	octaves	squirreled	tufts
cookstove	grizzled	quench	stubble	untamed
descending	irritated	revue	stupor	writhed

Section 3
Pages 96–149

average	festered	gullies	pandowdy	suffocated
bleary	forsaken	infantile	ponging	tempo
chaos	frail	jittery	scarred	thistle
duster	grit	moonshine	scuff	tracings

Section 4
Pages 150–189

crank	fleeing	knoll	plaster	rickety
divining	gummed	parcel	plunged	sparse
drenching	hometown	parched	procession	swarmed
featured	idled	pitching	puddled	whooping

Section 5
Pages 190–227

applied	cottony	latch	ringed	slat
betrothal	diversification	mottled	sassy	smothering
busted	drifts	nourish	shifting	soft-eyed
comical	flinch	reserves		

8

Vocabulary Activities

To help your students learn and retain the necessary vocabulary for *Out of the Dust,* engage them in interesting vocabulary activities.

Matching Game

Write the vocabulary words on index cards and tape them onto the chalkboard. Write the definitions of these vocabulary words on index cards and place them in a pile on a table. Divide your class into teams of four or five. Students take turns drawing a card with a definition. They then have 30 seconds to match the definition with the vocabulary word. If they match it correctly, they get a point. If they do not, the definition goes to the bottom of the pile and the next team takes a turn.

Pass-Along Story

Have each student write the beginning of a story. A vocabulary word must be used in a sentence in the story. After about five minutes of writing, the students exchange their stories and begin adding to the story started by the other student. They must also use a vocabulary word somewhere in the section they are writing. Continue the process, exchanging at least three or four more times. It is interesting to see how each story ends up!

Vocabulary Baseball

Divide your class into two teams and set up a baseball diamond, provide a soft ball that can be thrown in the classroom. The batter either spells or gives the definition of the word given to him or her by the pitcher. If the batter answers correctly, the pitcher throws the ball. The batter uses his or her hand as a bat. An incorrect answer counts as an out. Switch teams when there are three outs.

Puzzles

Have each student create a word search or crossword puzzle, using vocabulary words from the book. Reproduce the puzzles to share with the entire class.

Vocabulary Charades

Divide the class into teams and have individual students act out the vocabulary words.

Word Shift

Review parts of speech with your students by having each student group the vocabulary words into categories of nouns (common and proper), adjectives, adverbs, and verbs. Challenge students by asking them to change as many words as possible by adding suffixes. Ask them to identify the parts of speech of the newly created words. For example: nourish (verb), nourishment (noun).

Compact Vocabulary

Have students practice their writing skills by creating sentences and paragraphs in which multiple vocabulary words are used correctly. Ask them to share their sentences and paragraphs with the class.

Show What You Know!

Answer the following questions about pages 1–51.

1. How did Billie Jo get her name? What does she look like?

_____

_____

2. Who is Livie? Where is she going?

_____

_____

3. Who is Arley Wanderdale? What does he ask Billie Jo to do?

_____

_____

4. What is Billie Jo's family's routine when they sit to eat?

_____

_____

5. What makes Billie Jo feel as "foul as maggoty stew"?

_____

_____

6. What is Ma's suggestion about what to do when the wheat will not grow?

_____

_____

7. When the rain finally comes down hard and fast, why aren't the people happy?

_____

_____

8. What is Ma nursing and trying to protect through the drought?

_____

_____

9. What word do all the songs that Billie Jo picks to play with Arley and the Black Mesa Boys contain?

_____

_____

10. Write a one-paragraph summary of the major events that happened in this section. Use the back of this paper.

Apple Recipes

Billie Jo's mother took care of her apple trees. They were her pride and joy, and they became a symbol of hope in the midst of the dust. Despite the harsh environment, the apple trees bloomed. Billie Jo anxiously anticipated the day when they could use the apples to make pies, sauce, puddings, dumplings, cake, and cobbler. Try some of these old-fashioned recipes for apples.

Apple Sauce (about three cups)

4 medium cooking apples, peeled, cored

$^1/_2$ cup (120 mL) water

$^1/_2$ cup (120 mL) packed brown sugar or granulated sugar

$^1/_4$ teaspoon (1 mL) cinnamon

$^1/_8$ teaspoon (.5 mL) nutmeg

Cut the apples into fourths. Heat apples and water to boiling over medium heat. Reduce heat and simmer uncovered until tender, five to ten minutes. Stir occasionally to break up apples. Stir in remaining ingredients. Heat to boiling; boil and stir one minute.

Apple Dumplings

Pie pastry for an 8-inch (20 cm) two-crust pie

6 baking apples, peeled and cored

3 tablespoons (45 mL) raisins

3 tablespoons (45 mL) chopped nuts

2 cups (480 mL) packed brown sugar

1 cup (240 mL) water

Heat oven to 425° F (218.3° C). Roll two-thirds of pie pastry into a 14-inch (36 cm) square and cut it into four squares. Roll remaining pastry into a rectangle, 14 x 7 inches (36 x 18 cm), and cut it into two squares. Place an apple on each square. Mix the raisins and nuts and fill each apple with the mixture. Moisten the corners of the pastry squares. Bring two opposite corners up over apple and pinch. Repeat with the remaining corners, pinching the edges of the pastry to seal. Place dumplings in ungreased baking dish. Combine the brown sugar and water and heat it to boiling. Carefully pour it around the dumplings. Bake, spooning the brown sugar and water mixture over the dumplings two or three times, until the crust is golden and apples are tender (about 40 minutes). Serve with whipped cream, if desired.

Apple Crisp

4 cups (960 mL) peeled, sliced, tart apples

$^2/_3$ to $^3/_4$ cup (160 to 180 mL) packed brown sugar

$^1/_2$ cup (120 mL) flour

$^1/_2$ cup (120 mL) oatmeal

$^3/_4$ teaspoon (3.75 mL) cinnamon

$^3/_4$ teaspoon (3.75 mL) nutmeg

$^1/_3$ cup (80 mL) margarine, softened

Heat oven to 375° F (190.5° C). Arrange apples in greased square pan. Mix remaining ingredients; sprinkle over apples. Bake until topping is golden brown and apples are tender, about 30 minutes. Serve warm, if desired, with whipped cream or ice cream.

Extensions

- What is your favorite kind of apple? Research to find out how many different types of apples there are and where they come from. What are some of your favorite apple recipes?
- How nutritious are apples? Research to learn the benefits of eating apples.

Creative Problem Solving

Each of us has problems to deal with on a daily basis. Some of them are more difficult to solve than others and require using resources like time, money, family members, skills, or experience. Often these resources are limited or nonexistent, making the solution more difficult.

This was a common experience during the Depression. Many people were without food to feed their families, without jobs to earn money, far from family they could turn to for help, and without the skills to care for their families in this time of need. It was critical for people to become more creative at solving their problems. Listed below are some problems that need solving. Work with a group to come up with some creative solutions to these problems. Ask one member of your group to record your answers. When finished, meet together as a class to share these creative solutions.

- It is Thanksgiving Day and you have a lot of company visiting to eat the big dinner at your home. Halfway through the preparations of dinner, a water pipe breaks and water begins shooting everywhere. The water has to be turned off. What do you do on this holiday with a house full of guests?

- You have plans to go and watch a movie tonight. You have made arrangements for many friends to come with you. As you get ready to walk out the door, your mom reminds you that you had promised another family that you would baby-sit for them tonight. What do you do?

- You got in a fight with your best friend. He thinks that you do not like him as much anymore. He tells you that you are always hanging out with somebody else. You explain to your friend that this is not true. You promise to meet him after school today to hang out together. After school you are invited to play basketball with a popular group of students. You are excited. You forget all about your promise to your friend until you see him walking into the gym two hours later. What do you do?

- You are sitting down with your family for a discussion about family problems. You are informed that your dad has just been laid off from his job. This is just three weeks before the last payment of your fee to attend Space Camp in the summer is due. You have been planning this trip for months. What do you do?

- You are excited to be invited on a trip with friends to see the Grand Canyon. When you get home, you realize that your parents have already planned a family trip to see your dying grandfather that same weekend. What do you do?

12

Startling Statistics

Use the line graph below to help answer the questions at the bottom of the page.

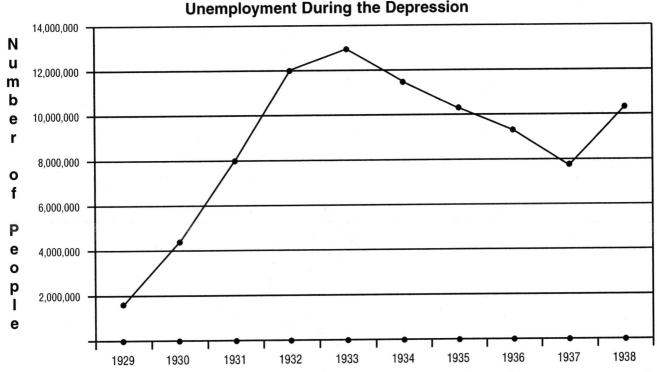

1. What is the title of the graph? In what year were the greatest number of people unemployed? In what year during the Depression was the number of unemployed people the lowest? What event signaled the beginning of the Depression? When did it occur? _____

_____

2. In which two years were there approximately the same number of unemployed people? About how many people were unemployed in those years? _____

3. What is the average rate of unemployment for the years shown on the graph? _____

4. How many Americans were unemployed in 1936? 1937? 1938? _____

5. What do you think was happening in 1937 to cause the number of unemployed to decrease? What do you think caused unemployment to increase in 1938? Use a separate piece of paper or the back of this page to give your answer.

6. Use the information from the graph above to create a bar graph on a separate piece of paper. In your opinion, which graph best displays the information?

Bonus: In what year did President Roosevelt begin his New Deal? Did it have an immediate effect on unemployment?_____

Extension: Research various New Deal programs and the years in which they took effect. Compare the years of the programs to information on the graph. Can you draw any conclusions about which programs were most effective in ending unemployment?

Reading Response Journals

Throughout this unit, students will be asked to write down their thoughts, ideas, guesses, feelings, opinions, and suggestions. Getting students to write these down is crucial to their making the connections in their lives to the history they are studying.

These journal entries should flow naturally from the lessons taught or from class discussions. They are most successful when the students see them as an opportunity to explore and create ideas. Try to create a positive feeling toward journal writing. Vary the time in the lesson that students write in their journals. The journal entries may be made at the beginning, during, or at the end of a lesson. Using a variety of times keeps the journal from becoming mundane.

Directions

Each student will need a notebook to use as a journal. Students may also create their own journals, using lined and unlined notebook paper with construction paper covers.

Tell the students that their journal entries should be written as honestly and thoughtfully as possible.

Instruct the students to write the date at the beginning of each journal entry. Their opinions may change from the beginning of the unit to the end. Learning more information on a certain subject allows us to go into more depth and use critical thinking skills to solve problems and issues. Encourage students to share journal entries if they are comfortable doing so. Students gain ideas and insights on topics and issues from other students. Learning takes place when ideas are shared.

Journal Entry Suggestions: Here are a few questions that can be used in the student journals. Create other questions or topics based on student responses to the book.

- How do you think living with all the dust would affect how you would feel?
- Can you think of a time in your life when you felt as alone as Billie Jo did after the accident? What did you do?
- Describe Billie Jo's relationship with her dad. What do you think could be done to improve their relationship?
- Billie Jo seems to like Mad Dog. How do you think Mad Dog feels about Billie Jo?
- If you were Billie Jo's friend, what would you do once you learned of the accident? Who are Billie Jo's friends?
- Describe a time in your life when you felt like you needed to talk and you did not have anyone to listen to you.

Extension

Create a parent/student journal. Ask the students' parents or grandparents questions that focus on life and personal relationships during the Great Depression. Students will learn much from hearing the opinions and ideas of those who either lived through the Great Depression or had family experiences associated with it. This provides an opportunity in an informal setting to share feelings, emotions, and ideas across the generations!

Show What You Know!

Answer the following questions about pages 52–95.

1. Who is the wild boy? _____

_____

2. Describe the accident. What caused it?_____

_____

_____

3. What does Daddy do with the money Ma had squirreled away?_____

_____

4. What happens to the wheat and the apples?_____

_____

5. What happens to Billie Jo's baby brother? What does Billie Jo name him? _____

_____

_____

6. How has Billie Jo's relationship with her father changed? _____

_____

_____

7. What does everyone gather to see at Mrs. Brown's house in the middle of the night?

_____

_____

8. Where does Billie Jo's dad get a job? _____

_____

9. How does Mad Dog treat Billie Jo? _____

_____

10. On the lines below, write a one-paragraph summary of the major events that happened in this
    section. If necessary, use the back of this paper.

_____

_____

_____

_____

_____

_____

Depression Details

Choose a project from the list below that you would like to share with the class. Completing these projects will help your class get a more in-depth understanding of the Great Depression and the circumstances under which Billie Jo and her family are living.

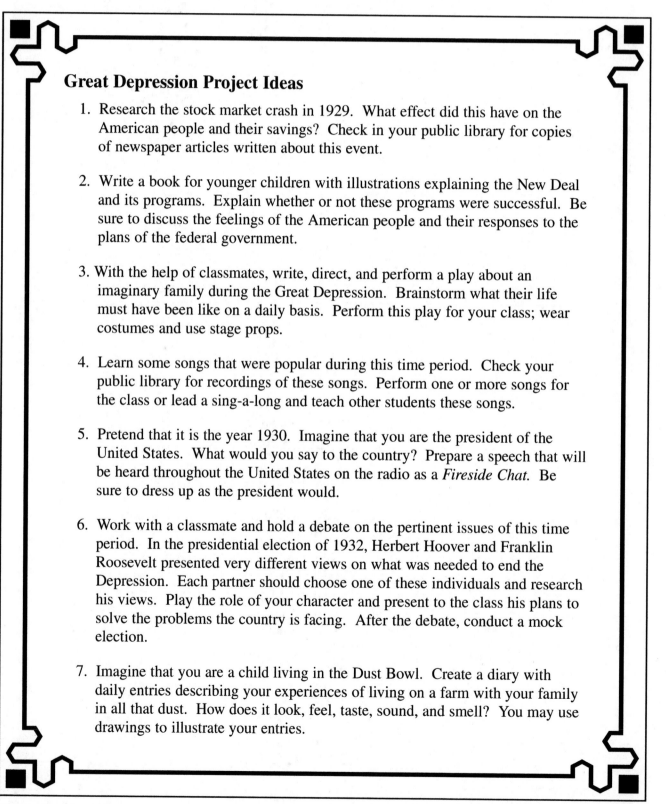

Great Depression Project Ideas

1. Research the stock market crash in 1929. What effect did this have on the American people and their savings? Check in your public library for copies of newspaper articles written about this event.

2. Write a book for younger children with illustrations explaining the New Deal and its programs. Explain whether or not these programs were successful. Be sure to discuss the feelings of the American people and their responses to the plans of the federal government.

3. With the help of classmates, write, direct, and perform a play about an imaginary family during the Great Depression. Brainstorm what their life must have been like on a daily basis. Perform this play for your class; wear costumes and use stage props.

4. Learn some songs that were popular during this time period. Check your public library for recordings of these songs. Perform one or more songs for the class or lead a sing-a-long and teach other students these songs.

5. Pretend that it is the year 1930. Imagine that you are the president of the United States. What would you say to the country? Prepare a speech that will be heard throughout the United States on the radio as a *Fireside Chat*. Be sure to dress up as the president would.

6. Work with a classmate and hold a debate on the pertinent issues of this time period. In the presidential election of 1932, Herbert Hoover and Franklin Roosevelt presented very different views on what was needed to end the Depression. Each partner should choose one of these individuals and research his views. Play the role of your character and present to the class his plans to solve the problems the country is facing. After the debate, conduct a mock election.

7. Imagine that you are a child living in the Dust Bowl. Create a diary with daily entries describing your experiences of living on a farm with your family in all that dust. How does it look, feel, taste, sound, and smell? You may use drawings to illustrate your entries.

Characterization

What do you know about Billie Jo? Discuss with a partner what you know about her up to this point in the story. How did you learn this information? There are three ways that you can learn about a character in a story. You can learn from:

- the author's description of the character
- the character's words and actions (and thoughts, it they are given)
- what other characters say about the character

The way an author shows you what a character is like is known as characterization. Find examples of each kind of characterization in the story *Out of the Dust*.

Write the name of a character from *Out of the Dust* on a small piece of paper or a self-adhesive note. Put this on the back of another student. Someone should also put a name on your back. Do not look at the name on your back. Now each student goes around the room asking other students a question about the character on his or her back. These questions should have a yes or no answer. For example, you may say, "Is my character a female?" or "Is my character old?" Continue this until everyone has discovered which character's name is on his or her back.

Speculate with a partner on the nature of the story *Out of the Dust* by discussing "What if?" questions.

What if Billie Jo were a boy? _____

_____

What if Billie Jo lived in New York? _____

_____

What if Ma never died? _____

_____

What if there were lots of children in Billie Jo's family? _____

_____

On the lines below, write two more "What if?" questions and exchange papers with your partner to answer each other's questions.

What if _____

_____

What if _____

_____

Extension: Create a new character to add to the story. Write a chapter that adds this new character and explain how things in the story change. Share this chapter with your partner.

In the News

Many of the events in *Out of the Dust* are based on events that happened in real life. This type of writing is called "historical fiction." Some of the historical information in the book could be used to write articles and features for a newspaper. Read the definitions of the parts of a newspaper below. Then choose one of the sections of the newspaper to write, using information from *Out of the Dust*. You may need to do additional research on your chosen subject. Write your rough draft on the back of this paper, then type a final copy.

News Article: The purpose of a news article is to provide facts and details about events. These articles answer the questions who, what, where, when, and why, (and sometimes how) about the subject. In a straight news article, the basic facts are presented in the first paragraph, in order of their importance to the story. Additional details and information are given in following paragraphs.

Editorial: This is an essay that expresses the opinion of the writer, usually the editor of the newspaper. Editorials are used to comment on events, state an opinion, educate or influence the reader, or to show appreciation.

Classified Ads: A wide variety of goods and services are listed in the classified ads of a newspaper. The categories include jobs, business opportunities, lost and found, housing for sale or rent, new and used goods and products for sale, services available, etc. Most newspapers charge a fee to people who want to advertise, based on the amount of space that the ad takes. Important details must be included, and abbreviations are often used.

Comics or Cartoons: These are hand-drawn pictures used to express an opinion or to amuse and entertain readers. Such features may be found in the entertainment, editorial, business, or sports sections of the newspaper.

Extension: Compile the articles and features created by the class to make a newspaper that might have been published during the Depression. Decide on a date for the newspaper, and brainstorm a name for it.

Through Our Own Eyes

Each of us goes through different struggles in life. Some of them seem to be more difficult than others. Billie Jo is going through a lot of things at once. She is devastated by the accident that causes her to lose her mother, her infant brother, and the ability to play the piano. There are stages of grief that most people go through when they have a severe crisis. Understanding these stages can help people see that their reactions are normal and help others to know how to help the individual. These stages are outlined below.

Stage 1—Shock and Denial

The individual feels numb during and immediately following the crisis. This can be merciful for the individual, and it can also be useful if one can understand what he or she is feeling.

Example: Billie Jo listens as the women clean her home after the accident. She cannot believe what has happened, and she hears the blame in the words of the women.

Stage 2—Anger

It is normal to feel anger along with grief. A person needs to be able to express his or her feelings. This anger is almost always temporary but may be exaggerated if one feels compelled to keep it inside.

Example: Billie Jo feels like she does not know her father anymore. She is angry that he is not opening up to her during this difficult time, and she blames him for what happened. She needs his support and love. She feels very alone.

Stage 3—Depression

The individual will likely feel depressed for some length of time after the crisis. Patience, love, understanding, and activity are good antidotes for depression. Frequently, others expect the person to have adjusted to the crisis when in fact he or she has not. The friendship of someone else who has had a similar experience and has adjusted is often very helpful.

Example: As Billie Jo goes through her box of collections, she is saddened and depressed by the memories and the fact that she misses her mom.

Stage 4—Acceptance

When the individual is finally able to talk about his or her experience realistically, he or she is on the way to adjustment. A person may still fall back into the different stages during the coming years, but those times will become less and less frequent.

Example: Later in the book, Billie Jo learns to move past the horrible accident by accepting her new life.

What types of things do you think would help Billie Jo survive this tragedy in her life?

_____

What things have you found helpful as you have gone through problems, disappointments, and trials?

_____

Show What You Know!

Answer the following questions about pages 96–149.

1. Who was Billie Jo's "mom" for the Christmas Dinner?

   _____

2. What was the President's Ball?

   _____

   _____

3. What did Billie Jo forget to serve her dad at their own Christmas dinner?

   _____

4. What did the government donate for school lunch?

   _____

5. Who were the "guests" at Billie Jo's school?

   _____

6. What song did Billie Jo play at the competition? What prize did she win?

   _____

   _____

7. What was the dust storm like when Billie Jo went to watch a show?

   _____

   _____

8. Who started night school?

   _____

9. What were many of the people in her town dying of?

   _____

   _____

10. On the lines below, write a one-paragraph summary of the major events that happened in this section. If necessary, use the back of this paper.

   _____

   _____

   _____

   _____

   _____

   _____

The 3-D Effect

Imagery is the use of words to paint a picture in your mind of what is taking place in a book. Authors often use imagery to create mental pictures for the reader. Choose a scene from this story and bring the mental image to life.

Begin by drawing a sketch of your scene on the back of this paper. Decide which parts of your sketch can be made three dimensional to give the scene some depth. Use the techniques below to achieve the 3-D look.

Pop-up Technique

Fold a standard piece of paper in half along the long side. Fold over the top corner, as shown. Fold it back and forth to make a crease.

Open the paper. Fold it in half so that the bottom edge lines up with the top edge, as shown. Close the card, pulling out the fold.

Inside the card, draw a picture, extending the drawing to the creased area. Cut out the shape on the pop-out section.

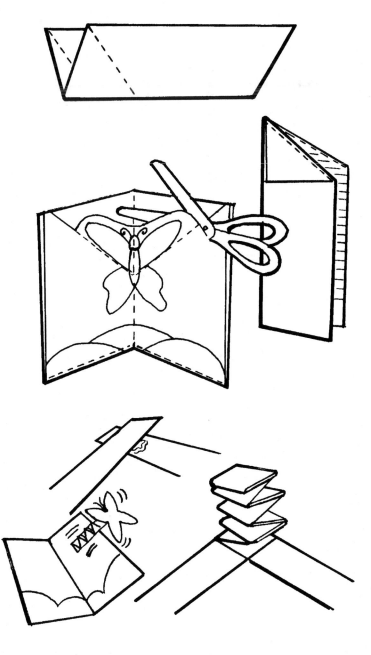

Folded Paper Technique

Cut two strips of paper. Dab glue on the end of one strip and put the other strip at a right angle to it, as shown. Press it down on the glue.

Fold the bottom strip over the top strip and press it down, making a crease. Fold the second strip over the first and press it down. Continue folding and pressing the strips until you reach the ends. Glue the ends together.

Glue one end of the paper "spring" to the background picture and one end to a cutout of the section of your picture you want to stand out on the page.

Draw your final version of the scene above on another piece of paper using paints, crayons, markers, or colored pencils. Add your 3-D effects to the finished picture.

Create-a-Story

Write a story cooperatively with two other students in the class about an item of interest during the period of the Great Depression and the Dust Bowl. One student will write the beginning, one will write the middle part, and one will write the ending of the story. (You may use extra paper, if needed.)

Meet as a group to discuss the topic and setting of the story and to decide which part each of you will write. You will need to meet again when the individual parts are finished to edit each other's contributions and to connect each of the parts together. You will also need to decide how to share your story with the class. Be sure to brainstorm together for the title of your story. Use the space below to plan and outline your story.

Title _____

Beginning

To be written by: _____

Details to include: _____

_____

_____

Middle

To be written by: _____

Details to include: _____

_____

_____

End

To be written by: _____

Details to include: _____

_____

_____

Map of Oklahoma

A good portion of the Dust Bowl took place along the panhandle of Oklahoma. Each of the places below was mentioned in the story *Out of the Dust*. Locate a map of Oklahoma in an atlas, encyclopedia, or other reference book. On the enlarged map of the Oklahoma panhandle below, locate and label the places and geographic features listed in the box. After you have finished labeling your map, you may wish to color it.

Keyes	Black Mesa	Felt
Guymon	Cimarron River	Joyce City
Beaver River	Texahoma	The panhandle of Oklahoma
Goodwell		

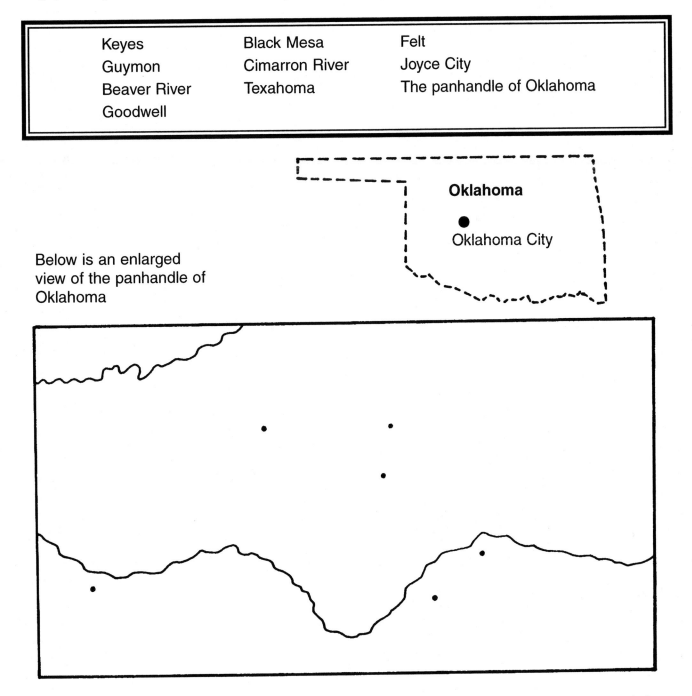

Below is an enlarged view of the panhandle of Oklahoma

Oklahoma

● Oklahoma City

Extension: Research to find out what the panhandle looks like today. Is the landscape green or is it barren? Are there trees, rivers, and other plants growing? Use an atlas to determine what the average weather conditions are like along the panhandle. Share your findings with the class.

Compare and Contrast

Compare and contrast yourself with Billie Jo. How are you alike and how are you different? What types of experiences do you share? How are your experiences different? Think of your community, your family life, your economic status, and your friends. List your similarities and differences below.

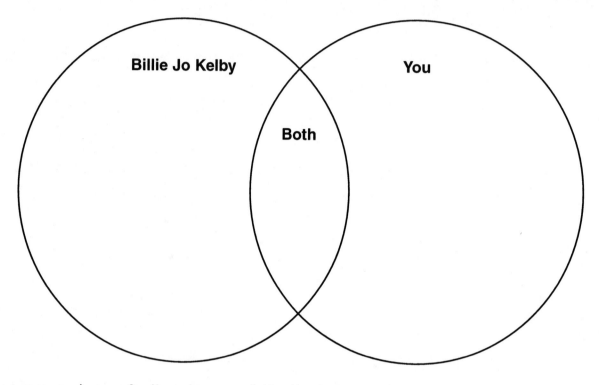

Select someone in your family or in your neighborhood whom you could interview about the Great Depression. This may be someone who is old enough to remember the Depression years or someone who has heard the stories of another who lived through the experience. Below are some suggestions for interview questions. You may add to this list. After the interview, draw a Venn diagram like the one above on the back of this paper. Compare and contrast your experiences with those of the person you interviewed.

Interview Questions:

1. How old were you during the Depression?

2. What do you remember about the Depression?

3. Describe your home and family circumstances.

4. Did you know anyone who lost his or her job?

5. What did you usually eat in one day?

6. What are some lessons our country learned from the Depression?

7. What surprised you the most about your experiences?

8. Tell about a very happy and a very sad time during the Depression. What good things came from your experience?

9. Do you remember what the newspaper and the radio said about the Depression?

10. When faced with a problem, what did you and others do to handle the problem?

Show What You Know!

Answer the following questions about pages 150–189.

1. What does Billie Jo's father have on his skin?

_____

_____

2. What catches fire in the town?

_____

_____

3. Who comes to visit and say goodbye to Billie Jo? Where is he going?

_____

_____

_____

4. What invitation does Billie Jo receive in the mail? What does she think of it?

_____

_____

5. Where does Daddy get the loan for the farm?

_____

_____

6. What happens when Billie Jo tries to play the piano at graduation?

_____

7. Who do they hear on the radio at the Joyce City Hardware and Furniture store? How does everyone feel about it?

_____

_____

8. What is left at the church? What does Billie Jo want to do with it?

_____

_____

9. What bones are they digging up out of the ground in Cimarron County?

_____

10. On the lines below, write a one-paragraph summary of the major events that happened in this section. If necessary, use the back of this paper.

_____

_____

Posters with Pizzazz!

Posters are often used to express ideas or to advertise movies, books, etc. A good poster combines pictures or art with a few words to convey a message. Choose a scene from *Out of the Dust* and use it to make a poster. Decide on a message that you would like to portray from this scene. Use the space below to plan your poster. Here are some tips that will help you in making the poster.

Making a Good Poster

Before you start the poster, think about the following questions:

- What is the purpose of the poster?
- Who is my audience?

Words: The main idea is the attention-getting message of the poster. The main idea should be in big letters. It can also be written with an exclamation point or question mark.

Detail information supports the main idea. Detail information is usually in smaller letters and can be separated by "bullets." Bullets are dots, dashes, or small symbols at the beginning of a sentence or short phrase.

Pictures: Art is used on a poster to get attention, to make the poster more attractive, to demonstrate the message, or to help explain the concept.

For your poster you may use pictures cut from magazines, photographs, symbols, or your own illustrations (draw in pencil first). You may wish to use boxes or decorative borders to organize your words and pictures.

Lettering: Always use pencil first when making handwritten letters. Make straight lines in light pencil first. If you use a stencil for letters, make light pencil lines to use as a guide. When using cutout letters, position them on your poster first. When you are sure they will fit, glue them down.

Plan Your Poster

Main Idea _____

Art _____

Detail Ideas _____

Style of Letters to Use _____

Make a rough draft by sketching possible layouts. Try to do at least two or three smaller sketches in pencil. Keep it simple. Too many words or pictures will make it seem too busy.

Wind Erosion

In this section of *Out of the Dust*, Billie Jo, her father, and many others get caught in a huge dust storm on their way to a funeral. Dozens of people stumble to a small home for shelter from the blowing dust.

During the Dust Bowl of the 1930s, millions of acres of farmland became useless as a result of the drought. When the winds came, they blew away acres and acres of topsoil. Farms, homes, tractors, and even animals and people were covered with sand dunes. This effect is called wind erosion. Working in small groups, complete the following experiment on wind erosion.

Materials *(These items are needed for each group)*

- sand
- large tray
- cardboard box
- wooden block
- sticks, blocks, rocks, fabric, or other materials

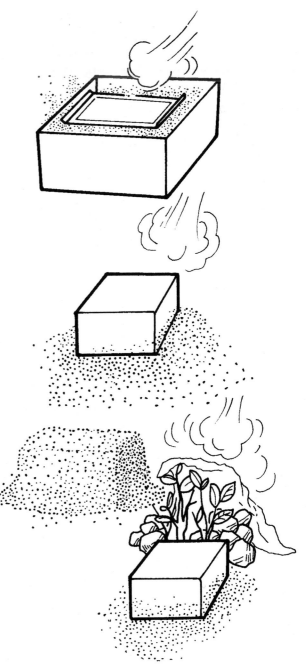

Procedure

1. Place a large tray inside a cardboard box. Cover the bottom of the tray with dry, fine sand. This is to represent the dust during the Dust Bowl. What will happen if a strong wind blows across this sand?

2. Have each person in your group take turns blowing from the same direction across the sand for a total of about 50 blows.

3. Your blows are like the wind. As it blows across the sand, it takes the sand with it. What do you think are the effects of this wind erosion?

4. Spread the sand back out again and place the wooden block in the sand. This block represents a house. Again, blow the sand toward the block for at least 40 to 50 blows. What is happening?

5. What can you do to stop the sand from covering the block? Use materials such as sticks, rocks, or fabric to make a windbreak.

6. Again, blow the sand toward the block. Did your windbreak work? Compare your windbreak with those made by the other groups. Did any design work? What makes a windbreak successful?

7. What were some of the other factors that hindered the farmers' attempts to prevent wind erosion?

Dust Pneumonia

The lungs are the critical part of the respiratory system. Without our lungs, we could not survive. Use an encyclopedia or other resource material to find the following parts of the lung. Locate and label the parts of the lungs on the diagram below.

Parts of the Lungs

| trachea | right upper lobe | main stem bronchus | left upper lobe |
| bronchi | right lower lobe | right middle lobe | left middle lobe |

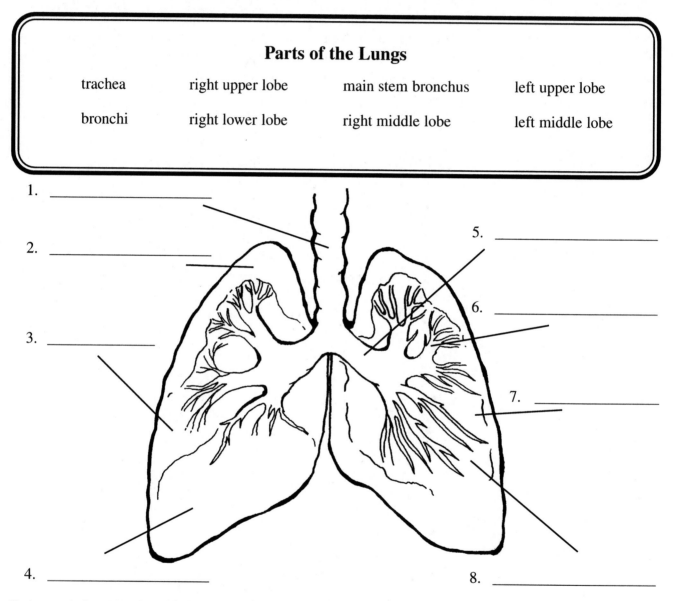

1. _____

2. _____

3. _____

4. _____

5. _____

6. _____

7. _____

8. _____

Pneumonia is an acute infection of one or both of the lungs. A bacterium, virus, fungus, or other organism can cause pneumonia. During the 1930s dust pneumonia became quite common in the Dust Bowl region. Because of all the dust in the air, it was difficult to avoid breathing in dust and other organisms. Symptoms of dust pneumonia include high fever, pain in the chest, difficulty in breathing, and coughing. Today bacterial forms of pneumonia are treated with antibiotics. Penicillin, the first antibiotic drug, was not discovered until 1939 and was not in general use until much later.

Extension: Do a research report on dust pneumonia, studying in more detail the causes, symptoms, and number of individuals who died of this during the Dust Bowl era. Share your findings with the class. Invite a doctor specializing in respiratory illnesses to talk with your class about the lungs.

In the Book or My Life?

Many of the stories we read have similarities to our own lives. Characters become real people to us because we can relate to them and to their experiences. What things do you have in common with Billie Jo? Read the following events that happened in the book. In the "In Your Life" column, write how these events are similar to experiences you have had in real life.

In the Book	In Your Life
1. Billie Jo is able to escape her everyday problems by playing the piano. Playing the piano helps her deal with her struggles.	1. What do you do when you get frustrated with life?
2. Billie Jo was sad to see her friend Livie leave. She could not talk much as they said goodbye because she had a lump in her throat.	2. Have you ever had to say goodbye to somebody whom you loved? How did you handle it?
3. Billie Jo's father wanted to have a boy instead of a girl when she was born. That was why he named her Billie Jo.	3. Has anyone ever wanted you to be something you are not? How did you feel about it?
4. Billie Jo's relationship with her dad is not a healthy one. They have a hard time talking.	4. Do you wish you had a better relationship with a member of your family? Why or why not?

Show What You Know!

Answer the following questions about pages 190–227.

1. What does Billie Jo do in the middle of the night? What does she take with her?

_____

2. Who does she meet on the train? What happens on the train?

_____

_____

3. Where does Billie Jo get off the train and call home?

_____

4. What does Billie Jo think about her running away experience?

_____

_____

5. Who does Daddy promise to go see? What does he do for Daddy?

_____

_____

6. Who is Louise? What does Billie Jo think of her at first?

_____

_____

7. What does Billie Jo tell Louise after the tenth time she came to dinner?

_____

_____

8. What are some of the things on Billie Jo's Thanksgiving list?

_____

_____

9. What is the feeling at the end of the book?

_____

_____

10. On the lines below, write a one-paragraph summary of the major events that happened in this section. If necessary, use the back of this paper.

_____

_____

_____

_____

Character Cube

Cut out the cube below. On each side of the cube, write characteristics and descriptions of the character named Billie Jo. What is she like? What are her problems/concerns? Characteristics and descriptions of Billie Jo might include nervous, dependable, judgmental, intriguing, laughs easily, etc. Think of as many others as you can.

Draw small pictures to illustrate your cube. When completed, fold the patterns along the dotted lines and glue the cube together using the tabs. Share these as a class when finished.

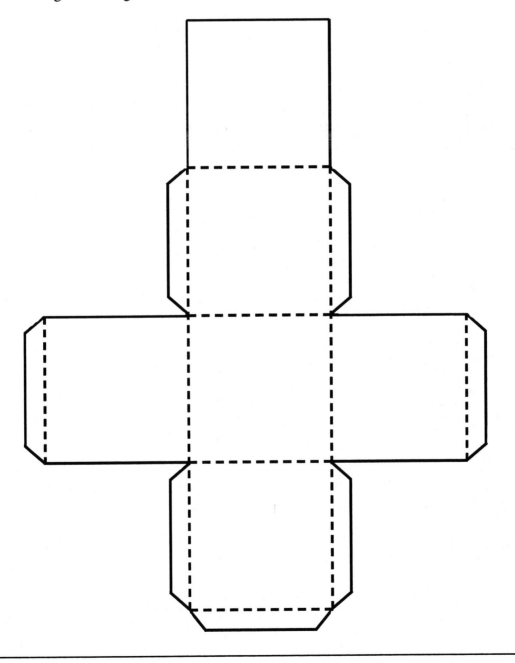

Extension: Play "Character Connections." Choose a character from the book. Act out his or her characteristics as your classmates try to guess which character you are portraying.

Lights, Camera, Action!

Working in a small group, select a scene from the book that you would like to produce as a play. One or more members of each group will be needed for each of the following tasks. Read the descriptions to help you decide which job you would like to do.

Present your completed scene to the class. If a video camera is available, you may wish to record each scene for future playback.

Production Roles

Screenwriter: This person is in charge of taking the book form of the scene and turning it into a script for a play with speaking parts and detailed descriptions of the scenery or setting. The script will need to be typed, edited, and copied for each person involved in the production.

Director: The role of the director is to organize the actors and the other individuals who are part of the production. He or she plans where the actors will stand during the scene and any actions they may make. The director guides rehearsals to help make the play polished and ready for an audience.

Actor: This is a person, male or female, who plays the role of a character in the production. His or her responsibility is to get to know the character from the book very well. The actor should dress accordingly and should be aware of how his or her character sounds? Actors also have to memorize their parts.

Costume Designer: This person is in charge of gathering costumes and deciding what each character should wear for the production. Each scene will need to be considered. Changing clothing can be difficult but can also bring validity to a scene.

Props/Scenery: The person responsible for the props and scenery will need to be busy working on these while the performers practice their lines. Scenery and props don't need to be elaborate to really add to the quality of the performance.

Writing in Free Verse

Karen Hesse, author of *Out of the Dust*, chose to write this story in free verse. Free verse is a type of modern poetry which is not written in any special form and does not require rhyme or rhythm. Free verse changes how a story is told and adds more information on how people are feeling. Read the following descriptions of the same incident. Sample B is written in free verse.

Sample A: Jeff hit a home run.

Sample B: Jeff stood,

> firmly planted
> inside the batter's box.
> With a kick of his shoes,
> the dust flew into the air
> and sweat began dripping off his brow
> as the umpire shouted,
> "Batter Up!"
> The ball came whizzing straight at him;
> one could almost hear the buzz in the air.
> Jeff reached his arm back
> behind his shoulder,
> mustering all his strength.
> There was a loud "Whack"
> as the ball met the wooden bat.
> Jeff wasted no time heading for his trip
> around the bases.
> Jeff heard the crowd cheering
> as he felt the familiarity
> of home base beneath his feet.

Now try writing your own free verse. On a separate piece of paper, describe your first day of school.

Checking Your Free Verse Poetry:

- Check the title. Be sure it catches attention and adds to the free verse.
- Check the spelling, punctuation, and usage.
- Check the capitalization. In free-verse poetry, it is not necessary for the first word in each line to be capitalized. You might decide to capitalize only a few words for emphasis.
- Is the free verse-poetry written neatly and clearly?
- Check the ending—free verse should not fizzle and die. Leave a good impression.

Forgiveness

Karen Hesse, author of *Out of the Dust*, spoke in her Newbery Medal acceptance speech about the importance of forgiveness. She said, "Just as Billie Jo forgave Ma. Just as Billie Jo forgave Daddy. Just as Billie Jo forgave herself. And with that forgiveness Billie Jo finally set her roots and turned toward the future." (*The Horn Book Magazine,* July/August 1998, p. 42.) *Out of the Dust* is not just a story about the Dust Bowl and the Depression, but a story about forgiveness. We see the character, Billie Jo, finally come to some resolution in her life once she begins to forgive. What role does forgiveness play in your life? Answer the questions below.

What is forgiveness? Look it up in the dictionary and write the definition.

_____

_____

_____

Why is it important in our relationships to forgive one another?

_____

_____

_____

Think of another character or another book you have read where forgiveness played a role in the story. Explain what happened below.

_____

_____

_____

_____

How does Billie Jo's life change as she begins to forgive?

_____

_____

Research Activity

The Great Depression took place in the United States, from approximately 1929 to 1940. Select one of the topics below to research. These topics are events or people of the 1930s. You may also choose your own topic with the permission of your teacher. Once you have determined your topic, select a method of presenting your research from the list at the bottom of this page.

Great Depression Topics

Black Tuesday	Stock Market	Henry Ford
CCC	Herbert Hoover	dry farmers
FERA	Dust Bowl	The New Deal
AAA	Fiorello LaGuardia	Okievilles, Hoovervilles
TVA	Franklin D. Roosevelt	tenant farmers
WPA	Harold Ickes	Bum Blockade
FSA	Eleanor Roosevelt	migrant workers
bank holidays	dust pneumonia	Weedpatch School

Methods of Presenting Research

Select one of the following ways to present your research:

1. Write a letter to a friend as though you were living during the Depression. As you write, detail your experiences to display the information you have gathered about your topic.

2. Construct a time line of the events of the Great Depression. Remember to include only the important or big events. For each event, draw a little picture and write a brief summary of what happens. Remember to place your events in chronological order.

3. Create an imaginary person that lived during the time of the Great Depression. Write a historical fiction story about this person and their life experiences during the Great Depression.

4. Produce a typed report presenting your information. Be sure to proofread and edit your report. Design a report cover. Prepare a condensed portion of your report for an oral presentation before the class.

Book Report Ideas

There are numerous ways to report on a book. After you have finished reading *Out of the Dust*, choose one of the book report ideas to complete. Be prepared to share your book report with the class.

Mix and Match Game

Take 10 index cards. On five of these cards, describe an event that took place in the story. On the other five cards, draw pictures that correspond with the events. Take turns playing this game with another student. Mix the cards up and lay them facedown on a table. Students take turns picking up a card, looking at it, and trying to memorize its content and location. When a player picks up a card and knows where its match is, he or she can pick them both up.

Group Presentation

Divide into groups. Each group takes a different section of the book. The group then discusses its section and decides how to present it to the class. These may be presented in the form of a skit, puppet show, interview, poetry reading, or anything else approved by the teacher.

Out of the Dust Time Line

Make a time line of important events in the book. You may include historical events that occurred during the Depression as well.

It's in the Bag

Collect at least 10 items that have something to do with an event from the book. Place the items inside a lunch bag. Give an oral presentation on the book or a section of a book. Pull each item out of the bag and discuss how it relates to the book.

Child's Play

The book *Out of the Dust* was written for older students. Write a picture-story version of this book for younger children. You will need to edit it and draw pictures.

Compare and Contrast

Read another historical fiction book written during the time period of the Great Depression. Make a Venn diagram to compare and contrast the two books. Share your findings with the class.

True or False

This book report is like a game. Two teams compete by writing 10 statements about the book that are either true or false. The teams then read off their statements and have the opposing team say whether they are true or false. The team gets a point if it fools the opposing team.

The Disappearing Chapter

Write a chapter that might have appeared in the book but did not. You may write it for the beginning, the middle, or the end of the story.

A New Twist

Listed below are the elements of a story. Choose one or more of these elements and change it in the story *Out of the Dust*. For example, the setting of this story is Oklahoma. Change the setting by having it take place in California midway through the story. Write this "new twist" below. How do the problems and events of the story change?

Elements of a Story

Setting—This is the location where the story takes place.

Characters—These are the people who are part of the story.

Theme—This is the message that the story is portraying.

Plot—This is the story line.

Viewpoint—This is the person telling the story. Different characters might see and relate the same events differently.

Mood—The mood determines the overall feeling of the story. (Is it mysterious, happy, sad, angry, etc.?)

Climax—This is the culmination or turning point of the story.

(title of "new twist") _____

_____

_____

_____

_____

_____

_____

_____

_____

Memories from the Dust Game

Materials

copies of pages 39–41, the directions and playing pieces below (bottle caps, chips, or other small objects may be substituted), the suggested answers on page 48, one die

Preparation

This game is designed for two to four players. Divide the class into small groups to prepare and play the game. One student in each group should be designated to check answers.

If desired, print the question cards and game boards on colored paper or ask the students to decorate them with watercolor markers. For durability, glue the question pages, playing pieces, game board, and answer key to card stock. Cut out the playing cards.

Playing the Game

1. Place the question cards facedown in a pile. Each person rolls the die. The person who rolls the highest number goes first.

2. The player rolls the die and, beginning at Start, moves his or her marker ahead the number of spaces shown on the die. If he or she lands on a square that says "Pick a Card," the player must draw a card and answer the question. If the answer is correct, the player stays on the square. If the answer is incorrect, the marker is moved back two spaces.

3. Place the used question cards in a separate pile. The player to the right then takes a turn, following the procedure above.

4. Play continues in a counter-clockwise direction. The first player to arrive on the Finish square wins.

Playing Pieces

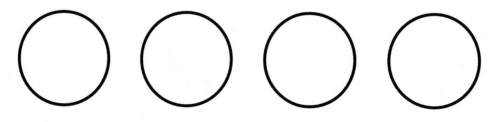

Extension: Create more questions from the book. Write them on cards and add them to the pile. Record the correct answer for each question on the answer key.

Memories from the Dust Game *(cont.)*

Question Cards

1. How did Billie Jo get her name?	2. Who is Livie? Where does she go?	3. What does Arley Wanderdale ask Billie Jo to do?
4. How does the accident happen?	5. What does Daddy do with the money Ma had saved up?	6. What does everyone gather in the middle of the night to see?
7. What makes Billie Jo feel "as foul as maggoty stew"?	8. What is Ma trying to nurture and protect?	9. What word do the songs that Billie Jo plays have in them?
10. How does Mad Dog treat Billie Jo?	11. What happens to Billie Jo's baby brother?	12. Who is Billie Jo's pretend mother at the Christmas dinner?

Memories from the Dust Game (cont.)

Question Cards (cont.)

13. What does the government give the school children to eat?	14. For what song does Billie Jo win third prize at the competition?	15. Who begins taking night classes?
16. Who is Louise? What does Billie Jo think of her?	17. Who comes to stay in Billie Jo's school?	18. People died of what disease that became common in the Dust Bowl?
19. What does Billie Jo's Daddy have on his skin?	20. Where does Billie Jo go when she runs away? What happens?	21. What does Daddy think about Billie Jo running away?
22. Why does Ma save Billie Jo's earnings?	23. What does Coach Albright want Billie Jo to do?	24. What is the purpose of the President's Birthday Ball?

Memories from the Dust Game *(cont.)*

	Pick a Card				Finish
30	31	32	33	34	35
Pick a Card			Pick a Card		
29	28	27	26	25	24
	Pick a Card			Pick a Card	
18	19	20	21	22	23
		Pick a Card			Pick a Card
17	16	15	14	13	12
Pick a Card		Pick a Card		Pick a Card	
6	7	8	9	10	11
Pick a Card			Pick a Card		Start
5	4	3	2		1

Letter to Karen Hesse

Now that you have read *Out of the Dust*, write a letter to the author, Karen Hesse. Some of the things
you might include in this letter are questions you still have about the characters or the events of
the story, things that you learned by reading her book, and comments or suggestions for the book.
Feedback from the intended audience is always valuable to an author. You might also ask her
about the background of this book and the history of how she wrote it.

Objective Test and Essay

Matching: Match the descriptions with the correct people.

Livie

Arley Wanderdale

Miss Freeland

Mr. Hardley

Aunt Ellis

1. _____ owns the general store.

2. _____ is Billie Jo's best friend but moved away.

3. _____ encourages Billie Jo to play the piano.

4. _____ is Billie Jo's teacher.

5. _____ invites Billie Jo to come live with her.

True or False: Write true or false next to the statements below.

1. _____ Billie Jo's Ma encourages Daddy to dig a pond.

2. _____ Mad Dog invites Billie Jo to go to Amarillo.

3. _____ Pete Guymon has a heart attack and dies.

4. _____ A homeless family comes to live at the school.

5. _____ Daddy goes to find Billie Jo after the bad storm.

Short Answer: Answer these questions, using complete sentences.

1. How does Billie Jo feel about playing the piano? _____

_____

_____

2. Describe Billie Jo's relationship with her father. _____

_____

_____

3. What happened to Billie Jo's mother? _____

_____

_____

4. What does Billie Jo do to "escape" her life in the Dust Bowl? _____

_____

_____

5. How does Billie Jo feel about Louise? _____

_____

_____

Essay: On the back of this paper, or on another piece of paper write short essay answers to these questions.

1. While they were living in the harsh conditions of the Dust Bowl, how did people continue to live and find happiness in their lives amidst such hardship and trials?

2. What role does forgiveness play at the end of the story?

Reflections

Explain the meaning of each of these quotations from *Out of the Dust*.

Note to the teacher: Choose the appropriate number of quotations to which your students should respond.

1. *I hollered myself red the day I was born. Red's the color I've stayed ever since.*

2. *When I point my fingers at the keys, the music springs straight out of me.*

3. *. . . we're all whittled down to the bone these days, . . .*

4. *. . . I glare at Ma's back with a scowl foul as maggoty stew.*

5. *It's being part of all that, being part of Arley's crowd I like so much, being on the road, . . .*

6. *I wish the dust would plug my ears so I couldn't hear her.*

7. *They only said, Billie Jo threw the pail of kerosene.*

8. *. . . he brushes his dusty hair back like my father, but he is a stranger.*

9. *I guess he gets the sound out of him with the songs he sings.*

10. *I dropped right inside the music and didn't feel anything. . .*

11. *My fingers leave sighs in the dust.*

12. *I tried to scare up something we could eat, but couldn't keep the table clear of dust.*

13. *We watched as the storm swallowed the light.*

14. *"It's best to let the dead rest," he says.*

15. *But mostly I'm invisible. Mostly I'm alone.*

16. *I go, knowing that I'll die if I stay, that I'm slowly, surely smothering.*

17. *"I didn't have half your sauce, Billie Jo," he says.*

18. *. . .when she smiles, her face is full enough of springtime, it makes her hat seem just right.*

Conversations

Work in size-appropriate groups to write and perform the conversations that might have occurred in each of the following situations.

- Billie Jo says goodbye to her good friend, Livie, at her going away party. *(2 persons)*

- Mr. Noble and Mr. Romney argue about who can get the most rabbits. *(2 persons)*

- Billie Jo asks her mother if she can go with Arley Wanderdale and perform in the Sunny of Sunnyside performance. *(2 persons)*

- Ma and Daddy discuss what to do with the farm. Ma thinks they ought to try a different crop. Daddy wants to stick with wheat. *(2 persons)*

- Billie Jo overhears the women of the town talking about the accident with Billie Jo and her Ma. *(4 persons)*

- Mad Dog tells Billie Jo how he got his nickname. *(2 persons)*

- Arley Wanderdale tries to get Billie Jo to do a show at the school after Billie Jo's accident and after the contest. *(2 persons)*

- Billie Jo and Daddy discuss the farm and Daddy going back to night school. *(2 persons)*

- Daddy and Billie Jo discuss the invitation from Aunt Ellis to come and live with her. *(2 persons)*

- Mad Dog comes to say goodbye to Billie Jo as he leaves for Amarillo. *(2 persons)*

- Billie Jo talks with the homeless man on the train to the west. *(2 persons)*

- Upon Billie Jo's arrival home, she and Daddy discuss their lives and the things they need to change and improve. *(2 persons)*

- Billie Jo tells Louise of their life together before she came along. *(2 persons)*

Bibliography of Related Reading

Fiction

Cochrane, Patricia A. *Purely Rosie Pearl.* Bantam Books, 1997.

Ducey, Jean Sparks. *The Bittersweet Time.* Wm. B. Eeerdmans Publishing Co., 1995.

Hamilton, Virginia. *Drylongso.* Harcourt Brace, 1997.

Hesse, Karen. *Out of the Dust.* Scholastic Trade, 1997.

Koller, Jackie French. *Nothing to Fear.* Harcourt Brace, 1993.

Myers, Anna. *Red-Dirt Jessie.* Puffin, 1997.

Porter, Tracy. *Treasures in the Dust.* HarperCollins, 1997.

Raven, Margot. *Angels in the Dust.* Bridgewater, 1997.

Thesman, Jean. *The Storyteller's Daughter.* Houghton Mifflin, 1997.

Nonfiction

Clark, Sarah Kartchner. *Thematic Unit: The Great Depression.* Teacher Created Materials, Inc., 1999.

Freedman, Russell. *Franklin Delano Roosevelt.* Clarion Books, 1992.

Galbraith, John Kenneth. *The Great Crash 1929.* Houghton Mifflin, 1997.

Hurt, Douglas. *The Dust Bowl: An Agricultural and Social History.* Chelsea Publishing Co., 1981.

JackDaws Publications, Ltd. *The Depression* (A packet of newspaper articles, signs, and other information from the 1930s). Golden Owl Publishing Co., Inc., 1972.

Shebar, Sharon, and Gary Lippincott. *Franklin D. Roosevelt & the New Deal.* Barrons Juveniles, 1987.

Stanley, Jerry. *Children of the Dust Bowl: The True Story of the School at Weedpatch Camp.* Random House, 1992.

Watkins, T.H. *The Great Depression.* Little, Brown & Co., 1993.

Videos

FDR: The Man Who Changed America. (1 hour) Phoenix Films, Inc., New York, New York. (212) 684-5910.

Franklin Delano Roosevelt. CRM/McGraw-Hill Films, Del Mar, California 92014. (714)453-5000.

The Great Depression. PBS Video, Alexandria, Virginia. (703) 739-5000.

The Inauguration of FDR 1933. (9 minutes) Blackhawk Films, Davenport, Iowa. (319) 323-9735.

Journey of Natty Gann. Walt Disney Home Video, 1985.

The Roosevelt Years Series. Films Incorporated, Wilmette, Illinois. (312) 256-6600.

Web Sites

The Web sites listed below have been reviewed and selected for use on the Dust Bowl topic. To access these sites, type in the listed URLs. Because Internet sites are constantly changing, you may prefer to use keywords like "Great Depression" or "Dust Bowl" and a Web browser.

The American Experience: Surviving the Dust Bowl (A teacher's guide to the PBS video with suggested lessons and activities to teach the Great Depression.) http://www.pbs.org/wgbh/pages/amex/dustbowl/teachers.html

The American Memory Library of Congress (This site offers lesson plans for teachers of American history.) http://www.cms.ccsd.k12.co.us/SONY/Intrecs/depwar.htm

Franklin Delano Roosevelt Web Site (This contains photographic images of the Great Depression and FDR.) http://www.corbis.com/special/FDR/

National Archives and Records Administration (A Web site sponsored by the National Archives offering Depression-era artwork, interviews, and more.) http://www.nara.gov/exhall/newdeal/newdeal.html

The New Deal Network (This Web site features more than 3,000 items, including photographs, political cartoons, original speeches and memos, and lesson plans for teachers about the Great Depression.) http://newdeal.feri.org

Answer Key

Page 10
1. Billie Jo got her name because her dad wanted a boy. Billie Jo is a girl with long legs, red hair, a wide mouth, and freckles.
2. Livie is Billie Jo's good friend. They have been friends since first grade. Livie and her family are moving to California.
3. Arley Wanderdale teaches music once a week at Billie Jo's school. He asked her to play a piano solo at the Palace Theater.
4. To set the table, Billie Jo puts the plates and glasses upside down and folds the napkin over the top of the fork, knife, and spoon. When they sit to eat, they shake their napkins and flip over their glasses. They joke and laugh about how much things are peppered or spiced because of the dust in their food.
5. When Billie Jo was asked to play the piano for the Sunny of Sunnyside performance, her ma said no because she thought she would miss too many days of school.
6. She thinks Daddy should put in a pond and try planting sorghum or cotton.
7. It washed the soil and the wheat plants away.
8. She is trying to grow apple trees.
9. They all have the word "baby."
10. Accept appropriate summaries.

Page 13
1. Unemployment During the Depression; 1933; 1929; stock market crash; 1929
2. 1931 and 1937; approximately 8 million.
3. 7–9 million people.
4. approximately nine million in 1936, approximately eight million in 1937, approximately 10 million in 1938
5. Accept reasonable answers.
6. Answers will vary. It may be easier to read the numbers on a bar graph.

Bonus: President Roosevelt introduced the New Deal in 1933. No, it did not have an immediate effect.

Page 15
1. He is a homeless boy without a job or food.
2. Daddy put a pail of kerosene by the stove. Ma picked up the pail, thinking it was water, to make coffee. Once she poured it, a small fire started in the kitchen. Ma ran out to get help from Daddy. Billie Jo, remembering the burning pail of kerosene, grabbed it and threw it out the kitchen door to prevent more fire. As she threw it, Ma was running back in and was hit with the kerosene and burst into flames.
3. He goes to Guymon and uses the money to drink all night.
4. When Billie Jo goes out for water, she sees clouds of grasshoppers devouring the crops. Nothing is left of the apples on the trees but the cores.
5. The baby brother dies soon after birth. Billie Jo names him Franklin, after President Roosevelt.
6. They hardly talk. Daddy does not even seem to notice that Billie Jo is there. Their relationship is strained and

distant.
7. People gather to see Mrs. Brown's cereus plant.
8. Her father is hired at Wireless Power.
9. He does not treat her like a poor motherless thing, he does not seem to notice her deformed hands, and he treats her like Billie Jo Kelby.
10. Accept appropriate summaries.

Page 20
1. Her teacher, Miss Freeland, is her "mom" at the Christmas dinner.
2. It is a dance held in town to celebrate President Roosevelt's birthday.
3. She forgot to serve cranberry sauce.
4. The government sent canned meat, rice, and potatoes.
5. The guests were a transient family that did not have a place to stay. The mother was expecting a baby. The family stayed at the school until the baby was born.
6. She played "Bye, Bye Blackbird" and won third prize.
7. It was so thick and heavy that she could barely see in front of her. She could not see where she was going and bumped into a box in front of her, scraping her knee. She had to keep spitting out mud, covering her mouth and clamping her nose shut. Her daddy came out in the storm looking for her.
8. Daddy started taking classes at night school.
9. They were dying of dust pneumonia.
10. Accept appropriate summaries.

Page 23

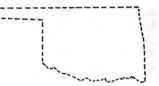

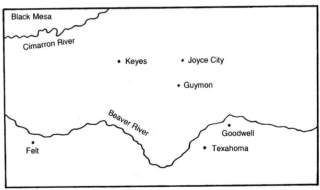

Page 25
1. He has raised spots that they think might be skin cancer.
2. Three boxcars in the train yard catch fire.
3. Mad Dog comes to say goodbye. He is leaving for Amarillo to sing on the radio.
4. Aunt Ellis invites Billie Jo to come and live in Amarillo. Billie Jo does not want to live with her aunt.
5. He gets the loan from the federal government.
6. She cannot play. Her hands will not work. She has to walk off stage.
7. They hear Mad Dog. Everyone is so excited and proud.

Answer Key *(cont.)*

Page 25 *(cont.)*

8. A baby is abandoned at the church. Billie Jo wants to take the baby home to live with her and her Daddy.
9. They find dinosaur bones in Cimarron county.
10. Accept appropriate summaries.

Page 28

1. trachea
2. right upper lobe
3. right middle lobe
4. right lower lobe
5. main stem bronchus
6. bronchi
7. left upper lobe
8. left middle lobe

Page 30

1. She runs away from home with only a few biscuits.
2. She meets a man who has left his family. He tells her the sad story of not being able to provide for them. He takes her biscuits and leaves his family picture with her.
3. She gets off in Flagstaff, Arizona.
4. She realizes that running away is no better. She learns that each of them needs to make changes and that they need to try harder.
5. He promises to see Doc Rice, who cuts away the raised bumps in his skin.
6. Louise is a lady who Daddy meets at night school. Although she does not intend to, Billie Jo finds herself liking Louise. Billie Jo hopes that Louise does not crowd her out of her Daddy's life.
7. She tells her all about her Ma and about their life. She shares her feelings about why she ran away and how she would love to play the piano again when she is ready.
8. Some of the things on her list are Daddy's smile, the whistle of gophers, the smell of grass, the spicy earth, Louise, food without dust, Daddy's hole staying full of water, etc. *(See page 220 of the book for the complete list.)*
9. There is a feeling of hope, renewal, recommitment, and forgiveness.
10. Accept appropriate summaries.

Pages 39–40

1. Her father wanted a son.
2. Livie is Billie Jo's friend. She and her family leave Oklahoma for California.
3. Arley Wanderdale asks Billie Jo to play piano at the Palace Theater.
4. Ma mistakes a pail of kerosene for water and it catches fire. Trying to save the house, Billie Jo throws the flaming pail out the door. The burning oil splashes Ma, and her clothing ignites.
5. He uses it to go drinking.
6. Everyone gathers to see Mrs. Brown's night-blooming cereus plant.
7. Ma refuses to let Billie Jo miss school to play piano for Arley Wanderdale's show.

8. Ma nurtures two apple trees.
9. The songs that Billie Jo plays have the word "baby" in them.
10. Mad Dog treats Billie Jo as someone he knows.
11. Billie Jo's baby brother dies.
12. Miss Freeland is Billie Jo's pretend mother at the Christmas dinner.
13. The government gives the school children canned meat, rice, and potatoes.
14. Billie Jo wins third prize at the competition for playing "Bye, Bye Blackbird."
15. Billie Jo's father begins taking night classes.
16. Louise is Daddy's lady friend. Billie Jo likes Louise.
17. A migrant family comes to stay in Billie Jo's school.
18. Many people died of dust pneumonia.
19. Billie Jo's Daddy has cancerous bumps on his skin.
20. Billie Jo takes the train, intending to go to California. She reaches Arizona and decides to come home after talking to a homeless man.
21. Daddy understands why Billie Jo tried to run away and says that he thought of doing it when he was a boy.
22. Ma saves the money to send Billie Jo away to school in the future.
23. Before the accident he wants her to play basketball but does not ask after her hands are burned.
24. Held in honor of President Roosevelt, the birthday ball raises money for infantile paralysis.

Page 43

Matching

1. Mr. Hardley
2. Livie
3. Arley Wanderdale
4. Miss Freeland
5. Aunt Ellis

True/False

1. True
2. False
3. False
4. True
5. True

Short Answer

1. Billie Jo loves to play the piano. Until her accident, that was what she loved to spend her time doing. After the accident, she could not play because of the pain and damage to her hands. It was very hard for her.
2. Billie Jo and her father do not have a very good relationship. They barely talk and her father does not seem to acknowledge her existence and her needs.
3. She caught on fire when Billie Jo accidentally threw a pail of kerosene at her. She probably died of complications from the burns to her body and, after such a trauma, giving birth to her baby.
4. She runs away. She feels she can no longer live that way.
5. At first she is hesitant to accept Louise, but Louise is easy to like and brings happiness back to their home. Billie Jo begins to open up and share her life with Louise.